GROUND BREAKERS
BLACK MUSICIANS

KENDRICK LAMAR

by Joyce Markovics

CHERRY LAKE PRESS
Ann Arbor, Michigan

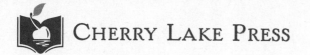
CHERRY LAKE PRESS

Published in the United States of America by Cherry Lake Publishing
Ann Arbor, Michigan
www.cherrylakepublishing.com

Reading Adviser: Beth Walker Gambro, MS, Ed., Reading Consultant, Yorkville, IL
Content Adviser: Michael Kramer, PhD, Music Historian
Book Designer: Ed Morgan

Photo Credits: © Tsuni/USA/Alamy Stock Photo, cover and title page; © Piero Cruciatti/Alamy Stock Photo, 5; © Matt Gush/ Shutterstock, 6; © AFF/Alamy Stock Photo, 7; © Kobby Dagan/Shutterstock, 8; Wikimedia Commons/Mick Taylor, 9 top; Wikimedia Commons, 9 bottom; © ZUMA Press, Inc./Alamy Stock Photo, 10; Wikimedia Commons, 11; © Zoonar GmbH/Alamy Stock Photo, 12; © Jamie Lamor Thompson/Shutterstock, 13; © Christian Bertrand/Shutterstock, 14; © AFF/Alamy Stock Photo, 15; © Christian Bertrand/Shutterstock, 16; © Jim Ruymen/Alamy Stock Photo, 17; Wikimedia Commons/Kenny Sun, 18; © ADREES LATIF/Alamy Stock Photo, 19; © Featureflash Photo Agency/Shutterstock, 21; freepik.com, 22.

Cherry Lake Press is an imprint of Cherry Lake Publishing Group.

Library of Congress Cataloging-in-Publication Data

Names: Markovics, Joyce L., author.
Title: Kendrick Lamar / by Joyce Markovics.
Description: Ann Arbor, Michigan : Cherry Lake Publishing, 2023. | Series: Groundbreakers: Black musicians | Includes bibliographical references and index. | Audience: Grades 4-6
Identifiers: LCCN 2023003488 (print) | LCCN 2023003489 (ebook) | ISBN 9781668927830 (hardcover) | ISBN 9781668928882 (paperback) | ISBN 9781668930359 (epub) | ISBN 9781668931837 (pdf) | ISBN 9781668933312 (kindle edition) | ISBN 9781668934791 (ebook)
Subjects: LCSH: Lamar, Kendrick, 1987—Juvenile literature. | Rap musicians—United States—Biography—Juvenile literature.
Classification: LCC ML3930.L136 M37 2023 (print) | LCC ML3930.L136 (ebook) | DDC 782.421649092 [B]—dc23/eng/20230125
LC record available at https://lccn.loc.gov/2023003488
LC ebook record available at https://lccn.loc.gov/2023003489

Note from publisher: Websites change regularly, and their future contents are outside of our control. Supervise children when conducting any recommended online searches for extended learning opportunities.

CONTENTS

THIS IS KENDRICK

Best-selling rap artist Kendrick Lamar is a master storyteller. "His work is more than merely brilliant; it is magic," said writer Toni Morrison. Kendrick uses music to explore the beauty and darkness of life. He raps about his own struggles and what it means to be a Black American. He also speaks up for **racial equality**. As one of the most influential hip-hop artists of all time, Kendrick is still breaking ground.

"LIVE YOUR LIFE, LIVE IT RIGHT. BE DIFFERENT, DO DIFFERENT THINGS."
–KENDRICK LAMAR

Kendrick Lamar, the groundbreaking rapper, songwriter, and producer

Kendrick Lamar has received many awards. He has won Grammys and the Pulitzer Prize—one of the highest achievements for an artist.

EARLY LIFE

On June 17, 1987, Kendrick Lamar Duckworth was born in Compton, California. His parents, Paula and Kenny, worked hard to support their family. "I knew I was blessed with a gift of having both parents," said Kendrick. Compton was filled with families trying to make their lives better. Still, it was a tough city to grow up in. Gangs controlled many of the streets. **Violence** was common.

Compton, California, is a city near Los Angeles.

As an adult, Kendrick still remembers his Compton roots.

When Kendrick was 5 years old, he saw his first murder. "It was outside my apartment," said Kendrick. "It let me know that this is not only something that I'm looking at, but it's maybe something I have to get used to."

7

Kendrick was a small, shy, sensitive kid who kept to himself. He enjoyed riding his bike and popping wheelies. But in his words, he had to "grow up fast." Gang members were everywhere. Police could also be a threat. Some singled out and **brutalized** Black people.

When he grew up, Kendrick rapped about his experiences as a kid in Compton.

"BLACK AND BROWN PRIDE HAVE BEEN TAUGHT IN MY HOUSEHOLD FOR A LONG TIME."
—KENDRICK LAMAR

Kendrick remembers the afternoon of April 29, 1992. That's when **riots** broke out in and around Los Angeles. They happened after white police officers beat a Black man named Rodney King. Afterward, the officers were not punished for their actions. Kendrick and his dad saw angry mobs in the streets. The experience helped shape young Kendrick.

Buildings destroyed during the 1992 Los Angeles riots

Rodney King

After his trial, Rodney King brought a lawsuit against the city of Los Angeles for **violating** his **civil rights**. He won his case.

As a child, Kendrick began writing stories. "You could put all your feelings down on a sheet of paper," he said. Kendrick dreamed of being a great writer. His father said, "We used to wonder what he was doing with all that paper!" Kendrick challenged himself "no matter what I was doing," he said. "Since the first time I touched the pen, I wanted to be the best at what I do."

Here is Kendrick as a young man.

Music was also a big part of Kendrick's early life. At age 8, he saw the music video for Tupac's song "California Love." It inspired him. He loved rap, including "Tupac, Biggie, Jay. Your usual suspects," said Kendrick. His parents introduced him to other kinds of music, such as R&B, funk, and jazz. Kendrick started putting beats to some of his stories.

Kendrick attended Centennial High School in Compton.

CENTENNIAL HIGH SCHOOL

Kendrick **excelled** in school. His teachers saw his talent and pushed him. "School was pretty fun for me," he said.

MAKING MUSIC

In 2003, when Kendrick was still in high school, he made a full-length **mixtape**. He called himself K. Dot. Kendrick's **intricate** lyrics and rich, layered sound got him a recording contract. He released another mixtape called *Training Day* in 2005. That same year, Kendrick graduated from high school as a straight-A student.

Kendrick performing as a young rapper

Rapper Lil Wayne was a young star like Kendrick. He started his career at age 12.

Kendrick began performing with other rappers, including The Game. More people saw Kendrick's talent and skills. Lil Wayne, another one of Kendrick's rap heroes, took notice. Influenced by Lil Wayne, Kendrick released his third mixtape *C4*. "Lil Wayne is the greatest. Not only because of his music but also because of the **culture** he put behind it," Kendrick said.

In 2009, Kendrick dropped K. Dot and started using his birth name. He began working on a mixtape that would become the album *Overly Dedicated*. The great rapper and producer Dr. Dre heard the song "Ignorance Is Bliss" and wanted to work with Kendrick. "I had to really snap out of fan mode," Kendrick said about meeting Dr. Dre.

Kendrick enjoys connecting with his fans on stage.

"IF I'M GONNA TELL A REAL STORY, I'M GONNA START WITH MY NAME."
—KENDRICK LAMAR

Kendrick put his everything into his next album *Section.80*. "I'm going to put my best out," he said. The album dropped in 2011 to rave reviews. While performing at a concert that same year, Dr. Dre, Snoop Dogg, and The Game called Kendrick the "new king of the West Coast." Kendrick was floored.

Dr. Dre and Snoop Dogg on stage together. Dr. Dre also grew up in Compton and went to the same high school as Kendrick.

In 2009, Kendrick, ScHoolboy Q, and other young rappers formed a hip-hop group called Black Hippy.

In 2012, Kendrick signed with Dr. Dre's record label. He released *good kid, m.A.A.d city*. It was a nod to his childhood in Compton. The album quickly climbed the charts. The songs "Swimming Pools (Drank)" and "Poetic Justice" were smash hits. Kendrick was **nominated** for seven Grammy Awards. But he walked away empty-handed.

President Barack Obama said "How Much a Dollar Cost" was his favorite song of 2015.

"I'M ALWAYS THINKING. I'M ALWAYS MEDITATING ON THE PRESENT OR THE FUTURE."
—KENDRICK LAMAR

In 2014, Kendrick won awards for his single "i." It was included in his 2015 album. The album became a big success. It talked about **police brutality** and **racism** as well as life and love. **Critics** said the album forced people to think. They called Kendrick "the greatest rapper of his **generation**."

Kendrick worked with Beyoncé on a song called "Freedom" for her album *Lemonade*. They performed together at an award show in 2016.

"Alright" was the fourth single off of his 2015 album. Kendrick wrote it after a trip to Africa. Since then, the song has been used as an **anthem** for racial equality.

Kendrick continued creating music that wowed fans. In 2016, he released *untitled unmastered*. This album included unfinished songs from his 2015 album. The next year, he released another album. Listeners were blown away by Kendrick's sensitive and **vulnerable** mix of songs.

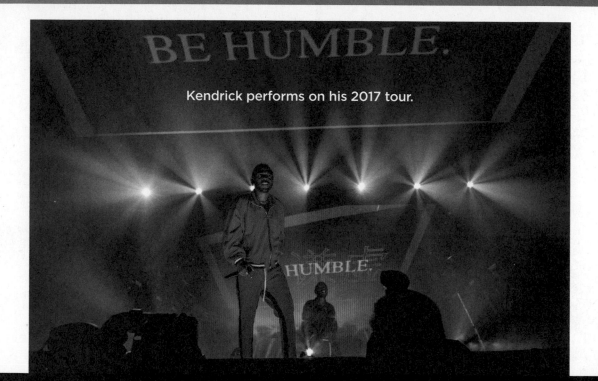

Kendrick performs on his 2017 tour.

"IT'S ONE OF THOSE THINGS THAT SHOULD HAVE HAPPENED WITH HIP-HOP A LONG TIME AGO. IT TOOK A LONG TIME FOR PEOPLE TO EMBRACE US."
—KENDRICK LAMAR

More awards poured in. One of the biggest was the Pulitzer Prize for music. "It was one of those things I heard about in school," Kendrick said. "But I never thought I'd be part of it." He was deeply honored. Despite the award and his fame, Kendrick has not forgotten where he came from. "As a kid from Compton, you can get all the success in the world and still question your worth," he said.

Here's Kendrick with his mom during the Pulitzer Prize ceremony in 2018. "I probably wouldn't be doing music if I couldn't find things to challenge me," he said.

Kendrick struggles with being famous. "I just remove myself," he said. "I like to look at old pictures and think of things from back in the day that kind of draws me back to where I came from." He has given millions to improve schools in Compton.

KENDRICK'S IMPACT

In 2018, Kendrick released the soundtrack for the blockbuster movie *Black Panther*. *Mr. Morale & the Big Steppers* came out in 2022. It was one of Kendrick's most personal albums. With each album, he looks deeper into himself. Kendrick said the hardest thing for "anybody to do is look themselves in the mirror and acknowledge, you know, their own flaws and fears."

Kendrick believes in sharing his gift with the world. "My whole thing is to inspire, to better people, to better myself forever in this thing that we call rap, this thing that we call hip hop," he said. And Kendrick is doing just that.

"AS LONG AS MY MUSIC IS REAL, IT'S NO LIMIT TO HOW MANY EARS I CAN GRAB."
—KENDRICK LAMAR

Kendrick Lamar has won countless awards and sold more than 10 million albums.

Kendrick Lamar has been with his partner, Whitney Alford, since high school. "That's my best friend," Kendrick said about her. They have two children together.

GREATEST HITS

Here are some of Kendrick Lamar's signature songs:

Alright

HUMBLE.

ELEMENT.

i

Swimming Pools (Drank)

The Greatest

Compton

Backseat Freestyle

Poetic Justice

Money Trees

* **Some of these songs include words that might not be appropriate for young people. Please talk to a parent or an adult before listening.**

GLOSSARY

anthem (AN-them) an uplifting song identified with a group or cause

brutalized (BROOT-uhl-ahyzd) attacked in a violent way

civil rights (SIV-uhl RITES) the rights everyone should have to freedom and equal treatment under the law, regardless of who they are

critics (KRIT-iks) people who judge something

culture (KUHL-chur) the ideas, customs, and way of life shared by a group of people

equality (ih-KWOL-ih-tee) the state of being equal

excelled (ek-SELD) performed very well

generation (jen-uh-RAY-shuhn) a group of people born around the same time

intricate (IN-trih-kit) complex or complicated

mixtape (MIKS-teyp) a recording on a cassette tape, CD, or digital medium, of music or songs by a hip-hop artist

nominated (NOM-uh-neyt-uhd) named for an honor or award

police brutality (puh-LEESS broo-TAL-ih-tee) excessive force and abuse by law enforcement

racial (RAY-shuhl) relating to the socially constructed groupings people are sometimes divided into based on the way they look

racism (RAY-siz-uhm) a system of beliefs and policies based on the idea that one race or group of people is better than another

riots (RYE-uhtz) out-of-control crowds of angry people

violating (VAHY-uh-leyt-ing) failing to respect

violence (VAHY-uh-luhns) swift and intense force meant to hurt or kill someone or something

vulnerable (VUHL-nuhr-uh-bull) open and able to be easily hurt

FIND OUT MORE

BOOKS

Levy, Joel. *Turn It Up! A Pitch-Perfect History of Music That Rocked the World*. Washington, DC: National Geographic Kids, 2019.

Richards, Mary, and David Schweitzer. *A History of Music for Children*. London, UK: Thames & Hudson, 2021.

Shea, Terese M. *Kendrick Lamar: Storyteller of Compton*. Berkeley Heights, NJ: Enslow Publishing, 2019.

WEBSITES

Explore these online sources with an adult:

Britannica Kids: Kendrick Lamar

Grammy Awards: Kendrick Lamar

Kiddle: Kendrick Lamar

INDEX

ABOUT THE AUTHOR

Joyce Markovics has written hundreds of books for kids. She appreciates the power of music to move and unite us. Joyce is grateful to all people who have beaten the odds to tell their stories and make great art. She would like to personally thank Kendrick Lamar for his music.